# CLARE

**A light that brightens the world**

by
John Paul Kirkham

*All booklets are published thanks to the
generous support of the members of the
Catholic Truth Society*

# CATHOLIC TRUTH SOCIETY
PUBLISHERS TO THE HOLY SEE

# CONTENTS

## Blessing of St Clare

May Almighty God bless you.
May He look upon you
with the eyes of His mercy
and give you His peace.
May He pour forth His graces
on you abundantly;
And in heaven
may He place you among His Saints!

## INTRODUCTION

The difficulty in writing about a person who was born over eight hundred years ago, is that often what material is available has either come from unknown sources or from stories that have been passed down and have become dramatically embellished or fictionalised, albeit with good intention. The life of St Clare as told here is both dramatic and true. After her death the Church authorities commissioned an official biography. The ascribed author was Thomas Celano of the Franciscan Order of Friars Minor who had previously completed the *The Life of St Francis of Assisi*. Celano was therefore a contemporary and his writings are based on all the known facts and the eyewitness accounts of the time, the living voices of those who actually knew and lived with Clare. In this little biography, I have strived to tell the story chronologically. The original medieval manuscripts tend to juxtapose certain events and add earlier happenings later in the text. This is the story of the founder of the Poor Clares, told "Franciscanly", through Clare's own life and writings, revealing her spirituality without much need of theological dissection or interpretation.

Throughout the text up to her canonization, I have chosen to call our "Great Saint" simply by her Christian name, Clare. This takes nothing of her sanctity away, but conversely draws us clearly into her light and reveals her in a more intimate way as one who we can easily know as a close friend and guide.

Final words of thanks must go to Sister Assumpta, Abbess of the Poor Clare Monastery at Arkley in Hertfordshire, and to Sister Chiara of Jesus at St Clare's Abbey in Darlington, and to both the above communities of sisters and many other Poor Clares who have assisted by prayer, in the writing of this book.

Previously I produced a contemporary translation of St Clare's own writings entitled *Clare of Assisi, Her Life and Message,* which can be used in prayer and for daily reflection and meditation, providing an oasis of calm in the busy world of today.

John Paul Kirkham
January 2006

## ASSISI AND CLARE'S BACKGROUND

### Medieval Assisi

Where exactly is Assisi? To say it is about halfway between Rome and Florence is all too vague. Italy is made up of nineteen provinces or regions and Assisi lies in the very heart of the country in the province of Umbria. The region's hilltop capital city of Perugia lies just a few short miles away across a valley to the west and is clearly visible from Assisi, whilst to the south lies Spoleto, and eastwards the cities of Norcia and Cascia, the birthplaces of St Benedict and St Rita.

Assisi like so many of its Umbrian counterparts, Todi, Gubbio, and Orvieto is situated on a plateau, commanding fine and distant panoramas. Arising from behind Assisi is the Appenine Mount Subasio that dominates the surrounding countryside with its lush soft green peaks and forests that capture the changing moods of the sun and the seasons.

Successive conquering emperors governed Assisi from behind the battlements of the stark and imposing Rocca Maggiore fortress. Those who found favour were Assisi's noble families, whilst the common people struggled to make their daily existence bearable by making a frugal living off the land or in the market place. A feudal system existed and it was common for neighbouring cities and towns to go to war against each other, making it dangerous to leave the confines of the city walls, as the surrounding lands were also the hunting grounds for bandits who would prey on any unsuspecting passer-by. In the year 1200 there was such a mutually shared hatred with Perugia that a war broke out that lasted nine years. This feudal system would however eventually crumble and the citizens of Assisi would form their own local '*commune*' government and from amidst the shadow of depression and hostilities a great ray of hope would soon shine forth.

## Clare's family

Clare's aristocratic and noble ancestry can be traced back to her paternal great-grandfather, Paolo, from the house of the Counts of Scefi who owned citadels and palaces in and around Assisi.

Clare's grandfather, an only child called Offreduccio, (this is the family name), owned a large house in the very fashionable area on the Piazza San Ruffino. To him three sons were born of whom Favarone would be Clare's father.

Favarone was a rich knight and was the master of a well respected house; he employed many servants and was a well known figure throughout the district.

Clare's mother called Ortolana, Countess of Sterpeto, was also well known and much loved by the people of

Assisi, being renowned for her works of charity and adherence to living a religious life. Ortolana spent a great deal of time travelling on pilgrimages to Rome and beyond, even as far as Jerusalem; all this in a time when a journey across the local valley would have posed some great hardship and risk. The name Ortolana in Italian means *gardener*, and she would certainly play a significant role in the cultivation of all her daughter's faith.

Favarone and Ortolana would have five children. Bosone, a boy and heir believed to have died early; Penenda the first daughter; Agnes whose baptismal name was Catherine and Beatrice were daughters number three and four. But it is now time to turn to the second and greatest daughter, Clare of Assisi.

### Birth to maidenhood

Giving birth for some can be a trying experience and in 1193 with her child's birth imminent, Ortolana felt very fearful and would often seek refuge in prayer in the Basilica of San Ruffino. Kneeling before the crucifix she prayed for a safe delivery and that all would go well in the expected childbirth. Ortolana described how in prayer she heard a voice saying: "Do not be afraid, woman! For you will safely give birth to a light whose rays shall illuminate the whole world" and on 16 July 1193 Clare's eyes saw the sun for the first time.

When it came to baptising the child in the same font that had witnessed the baptism of St Francis, Ortolana remembered God's comforting words and put forward the name Chiara, Clare which signifies light or to illuminate, hoping that this brightness foretold might in some way fulfill the promises of God's will.

Ortolana brought up her child well and instructed Clare in the faith and taught her how to pray. Clare's mother was certainly the guiding influence in the ways of God and the paths of virtue and her own pious life was a perfect example for a young girl to follow.

Clare's aunt, Bona Guelfuccio, a very devout widow, became her governess and confidant and quickly gained a deep insight into Clare's true spiritual nature and she would give Clare as much encouragement and help as was possible.

Assisi had its poor quarter and many ordinary people were starving and living in squalid conditions. Even as a young girl, Clare would make sacrifices for God secretly by denying herself the delicacies of the household meals and with the help of one of her aunt's daughters would send her own portions to the poor orphans and those who were in more need, indicating an early sign of her sanctity.

Clare loved to pray and would hide herself in the rooms of the house for hours on end in conversation with God. Not having a set of prayer beads, Clare would use a handful of tiny pebbles to count the prayers directed to the Lord. Immersed in a divine love, Clare gradually came to reject all worldly and earthly goods and regarded them as worthless things. Even under her softly tailored and rich dress garments she would wear a hair shirt. Her outward appearance would be as normal but internally she was wearing Christ already.

## Sudden move to Perugia

At the end of the twelfth century there was an uprising and most of the noble families moved to the rival city of Perugia. Perugia may have seemed a safer place and even Favarone was forced into exile and took the whole family with him. It was in Perugia that Clare would form a lifelong friendship with two girls, Filippa and Benvenuta who later would become amongst the first to follow Clare into religious life. The war between Assisi and Perugia would last another three years and then the temporary exile was over. Clare moved back home to her beloved Assisi.

Clare was now seventeen and had blossomed into a picture of great beauty. The family was respected and wealthy and her father had plans of a great wedding and therefore sought to contract a marriage with a suitor of aristocratic and admirable virtues. There was certainly no shortage of prospective noble husbands, but Clare would hear nothing of it. She not only refused, she would not even entertain any talk of weddings or marriage. This proved to be a great annoyance to her father and uncles, and when questioned further, Clare told them that all she wished to do was to preserve herself as chaste and commend her virginity to the Lord.

## CALLED TO SERVE GOD

### Clare, Francis and conversion

Assisi already had its own patron saint, St Rufinus (San Ruffino), who was an early christian bishop martyred for his faith. The large basilica dedicated to him, which contains his tomb and relics, had long been established in the upper part of the city and this same city was now about to witness the dramatic appearance of not only one, but two of the Church's greatest saints.

Francis Bernardone was born in Assisi in 1182 and was senior to Clare by eleven years. Like Clare, his family was well known and his father was one of the city's richest merchants. Francis as a young man was the life and soul of the many banquets and parties that he hosted; he craved adventure and dreamt of being a great knight of arms.

The time came for him to leave Assisi, waved and cheered off by the multitudes, dressed in the finest and most expensive armour and headed southwards towards Rome. The adventure was short-lived and no sooner had he left than he returned in just a few short days, a changed and different person. He took to wearing rags and wandering amongst the hills and countryside, living in a cave not far from the church ruins of San Damiano.

In 1206, whilst praying before the large crucifix in the crumbling church, Francis heard God's call, the voice that asked him to rebuild his Church and from that moment Francis would live the Gospel to the exact word; he would renounce everything and devote himself to God and to poverty. He even predicted in the not so distant future 'the coming of a community of Poor Ladies'.

News of his behaviour spread and many thought him an eccentric madman, as he and his disciples begged from door to door and town-to-town for scraps to eat. Even so there were a few who could discern a true holiness in how he acted, and Clare as a young teenager would certainly have known about this intriguing and faithful servant of God.

In 1209 Francis' Rule for his Order of Friars Minor received verbal approval from Pope Innocent III and he took to the road preaching. From the pulpit of San Ruffino in Assisi, his sermons were simple yet powerful and focussed on the Gospel: "that poverty, which was to possess nothing was to gain everything in God". He had a small number of followers, the first twelve "Brothers" of the Franciscan Order, that banded together in small makeshift huts next to the Church of St Mary, known as the Porziuncula, at the foot of the hill of Assisi. Clare was inspired by this new, radical way of life and with her friends she sought out this holy man, the founder of this new order who would become her spiritual guide and new father in faith.

There does not seem to be an exact moment of time that can be traced to Clare's conversion. In fact the journey it seems was already predestined from her mother's womb. On her return from Perugia, Clare continued to assist the poor and hungry and spent the rest of her time offering prayers and penance for the love of the crucified Lord.

Clare withdrew from the outside world and her rooms at home would be her secluded cloisters; Clare's life of prayerful solitude had begun. The only subject that she would converse about at home to family members, relatives and visitors, was God. News of Clare's piety and devotion to Jesus spread throughout Assisi and it would just be a matter of time before this maiden's fame to holiness would reach the ears of Francis himself.

At first however, it was Clare who had heard about Francis and she desired to see and hear him. Francis' mission was to warn against the folly of the world and to win souls for God's Kingdom. The words that spoke to him came directly from God as he wandered in the wilderness; once, after praying, he randomly opened the Bible at Matthew's Gospel: 'Jesus said, "If you wish to be perfect, go and sell what you own and give the money to the poor, and you will have treasure in heaven; then come, follow me"' (*Mt* 19:21). This was the pillar of the Good News that he preached to all who would listen to him. This was his way, his ideal.

Francis called on the House of Offreduccio and Clare would, with a chaperone, frequently visit him to listen to him make following Jesus so compelling. Clare would only leave the family home accompanied by her faithful friends or with her trusted Aunt Bona Guelfuccio.

Francis would reveal to her the emptiness of all worldly hopes and dreams. He told her what Jesus said: "Take nothing for the journey: neither staff, nor haversack, nor bread, nor money; and let none of you take a spare tunic" (*Lk* 9:3). This hardship, he said, could be rewarded by a vision of the eternal joys that lay ahead, and this caused her heart to ache with such yearning to become a bride of the heavenly King. She despised all vanity and desired to consecrate her body and soul to God alone. Over the next two years, Francis would guide Clare to new levels of spiritual awareness. When Francis spoke to her, it was with fervour of the love of Jesus; he exhorted Clare to focus her whole life, body and soul towards the love of Christ, to desire nothing and wish for nothing else; and to let nothing else please or delight her, other than the Creator, Redeemer and Saviour, the only true God. God had revealed to her the way: "If anyone wants to be a follower of mine, let him renounce himself and take up his cross every day and follow me" (*Lk* 9:23).

The seal was now set. The path Francis had chosen to follow would become the road for Clare as well, which would mean renouncing her life and choosing poverty. It was now necessary for Clare to discern how to fulfill God's privileged plan for her.

## Clare's flight from home

Clare had asked Francis for help in finding a way to fulfill her vocation and Bishop Guido of Assisi, who was a most faithful counsellor and devoted friend of Francis, was sought out to approve and advise the way.

On the day before Palm Sunday in 1212, Clare visited Francis and a dramatic plan was carefully put into place to remove her from the ills of the world. On 18th March, Palm Sunday, Clare went to Mass, as usual, at the Basilica of San Ruffino along with all the young girls, dressed in her finest gown. When the girls went up to the altar to receive their palms or olive branches, Clare remained transfixed to her seat. All eyes in the cathedral gazed towards her, in an atmosphere of expectancy and suspense. Bishop Guido himself stepped down from the sanctuary and walked towards Clare and gave her a palm. Clare took this as a sign that the time had now come and whatever was to happen would be directed by God's own hand.

The Lenten twilight turned to darkness and Clare, although nervous, put her plan into action. It would have been foolish to leave through the front door of the house as this led directly onto the main square. There would be those about who could recognise her or sound the alarm.

There was a side door exit but this was barred and sealed up. Clare was given the miraculous strength to remove and overcome this first obstacle in her path and, with the side door now opened, and aided by her cousin Pacifica, she secretly set foot out into the night. With the silhouette of Assisi's grand basilica behind them they fled first through the quiet side streets then down into the forested hillside. Past midnight, with only the moonlight as their guide, they descended to the foot of the valley where Francis and his brothers were waiting at the Church of St Mary of the Porziuncula, keeping a night vigil at the altar with lighted torches. As soon as they arrived, Clare submitted to the tonsure and her long, blonde tresses of hair were shorn from the crown of her head. Disposing of her worldly clothes, Francis attired her in the poor robe of a habit. After prostrating herself before the Altar of the Blessed Virgin, Clare left for the safety of the Benedictine monastery of San Paolo, just two miles away from Assisi.

It didn't take very long for Clare's family to discover what had happened. They were filled with grief and condemned the act as a betrayal. The extended family rushed to San Paolo to plead with their daughter to return home. They would have used violence to retrieve her but the monastery, as a holy place, was subject to the law and rule of asylum. The family refused to give up and pleaded with her to come home to be restored to the good life she was used to. When all reasoning failed they resorted to verbal abuse and threats. At this point, Clare publicly removed her veil baring her shaved head, and the family finally accepted that nothing would deter her from serving Christ.

A few days later when things had quietened down, Clare moved to another Benedictine monastery, San Angelo di Pansa on the slopes of Mount Subasio to the east of Assisi. She had only been with this new community for a short time when another sensational family event broke out.

It had taken just sixteen days for Clare's sister Agnes to decide that she too wanted to join Clare and follow in our Lord's footsteps. This came as no surprise to Clare as she had been praying continually that Agnes would come to join her. After losing one daughter, Favarone could not contain his anger any longer and this time, what seemed like an army set off to bring back Agnes at any cost. When the party arrived at San Angelo di Pansa they hid their rage by a cunning deceit to gain access to the convent. Having long since given up any hope of persuading Clare, their attention turned to Agnes. Agnes' refusal was too much and one of the knights brutally assaulted her. With punches and kicks, he dragged her off by the hair. The assailants lifted her up and carried her away and the undignified sight continued down the hill slopes. Agnes cried out to Clare and to God for help; her garments were torn to pieces and her hair was pulled out by the handful. Clare had fallen on her knees before God and pleaded for the release of Agnes. Suddenly the body of Agnes became so heavy that the party could not carry her over the small river. Even after calling for extra hands from the vineyards, her weight was so much that she remained rooted to the floor. Mocking this miracle, her uncle drew his sword to stab her, but his hand was gripped with a most intense pain which would linger long after this murderous attempt. Clare now appeared and begged for her half-dead sister to be released into her care. Realising any more attempts would be futile, they reluctantly walked away leaving the two jubilant sisters to their own means and God's destiny. In this way Agnes became the first follower of Clare in the church that Francis had restored and built with his own hands.

## SAN DAMIANO: THE EARLY YEARS

### A contemplative and enclosed life

The Church and monastery of San Damiano is a short walk down a steep incline just outside the eastern wall of Assisi. On the advice of Francis, Clare having already given her dowry to the poor at San Angelo moved into this bare and poor abode in 1212. It would be her home for the last forty-two years of her life. Confined to her tiny cell, cloisters, garden and chapel, Clare withdrew from the world and this self-imposed solitude became her heavenly nest on earth. It would be her place of silence, prayer, penance, poverty and dedication to all who wished to follow this strict form of religious life. Her mission was to pray and win souls for her beloved Lord. This community that was unique in many ways became known as the "Poor Ladies" of the Order of San Damiano (the Damianites).

Very soon the fame and sanctity of Clare spread through the whole region and it wasn't long before the community of two (Clare and her sister Agnes) would grow.

First came two of Clare's close childhood friends, Benvenuta from Perugia and Pacifica. Shortly after, many rich young maidens, inspired by Clare's holiness, gave up all they had to dedicate their lives to Christ. Mothers encouraged daughters, daughters encouraged their mothers, sisters extolled sisters, and nieces and aunts came to join the monastery. Outside the walls attitudes began to change; men swelled the ranks of Francis' First Order of Brothers. Married couples began to explore ways of adopting such a way of life in the home without being formally bound by monastic rules. This was in many ways an early form of the Third Franciscan Order (or Tertiaries). Although enclosed and set apart, Clare was now starting to fulfill the prophesy and enlighten the world from within.

As many girls and women discovered conversion to Christ, Clare sent out sisters to found new convents and monasteries throughout Italy and elsewhere. In her own lifetime, she would see one hundred and fifty houses of the Order spring up. Great numbers willingly followed this way of life, as a call to live simply, even more, a call to live the Gospel.

## The privilege of poverty

Clare wanted to live as a humble sister, preferring to be a willing daughter of Christ serving the other sisters, rather than to have any place of authority. It was only in obedience to Francis, her "holy father", and the local Bishop, that Clare reluctantly took the title of Abbess, an office she would hold until death.

Even so, as Abbess, Clare never shirked any responsibility; she would wash the hands of the sisters, serve the meals and waited on them at table. Clare rarely gave orders, preferring to do any extra work herself. She would willingly tend the sick sisters, washing them and their toilet-soiled clothing, never shrinking away from illness. When any lay sister arrived at the monastery Clare, on bended knees, would immediately clean and dry their feet. During the cold and freezing winter nights, Clare would remain awake tending the sleeping sisters beds by making sure they were always covered by a blanket keeping out the icy drafts of air. As Abbess she took full responsibility for the spiritual and moral guidance of her sisters through the example of a single-minded love of God, devotion to prayer, and acts of sisterly charity.

To live the Gospel meant living without any means whatsoever. All worldly goods had been rejected and the community would accept no money or possessions; instead they would rely on the work of their hands.

The Order was both revolutionary and unique in its practice of Christian values. Francis had written his Rule which the "Poor Ladies" followed: penance, following the Gospel, to live in the highest degree of poverty, to practice Christian love and to remain faithful and submissive to the one Holy Catholic Church. The sisters embraced all these ideals, but it was compassion and poverty that Clare is most remembered for.

In 1215 Clare petitioned Pope Innocent III. She wished to possess nothing but Christ and forbade her sisters from possessing anything at all. Clare wanted the title of her order to include the word "poor" and so asked the Holy Father for "The Privilege of Poverty". The Pontiff congratulated Clare on her great fervour and declared that no such request or privilege had ever been requested before from the Holy See. Indeed the fourth Lateran Council had decided not to accept any new rules and it was the Rule of St Benedict that was the norm. For any monastery or convent not to own any property was unheard of. However, the enlightened and inspired Pope granted this unique privilege to the extent that he wrote the opening lines of the document himself.

Later, in 1228, Pope Gregory IX tried to persuade Clare to consent to having some possessions, as he feared for such dangerous times and that the sisters may need help in the future. He went as far as offering some goods of his own. Clare, true to her way of life, resisted politely; and so Pope Gregory IX confirmed her "Privilege of Poverty", extending the Rule of Poverty to all the other monasteries of the Order.

Clare had renewed her vows to follow Christ alone and to acquire nothing. She was more content to receive the small morsels of bread that the Franciscan brothers had begged for, than to receive a whole loaf. This was poverty and it made her feel far more comfortable.

## Miracles of bread and oil

Francis and his Order had agreed to look after the spiritual needs of the Poor Ladies. Francis himself would visit from time to time but he had appointed a chaplain, (a priest) and two Questors (lay brothers) to look after the sisters' requirements. The two lay brothers were commissioned to collect alms for the Poor Ladies. There was a small hospice close to the monastery of San Damiano that was always inhabited by a small group of Friars, who would beg for food to sustain the community of sisters.

One day, it happened that only one loaf of bread could be found in the monastery. Clare told the sister in charge of the kitchen to divide the loaf in half, one half for the Friars and one half for themselves. Clare then asked the sister to cut fifty slices from the remaining half-loaf and serve them to the table. The sister told Clare that a special miracle of Christ would be needed to multiply that small piece of bread into fifty portions. The holy Abbess replied "Do what I say and trust in me". The sister went hastily away to comply with the request. Clare then cast herself at the feet of Jesus, her beloved spouse; while the sister was cutting the bread, the slices increased miraculously and there was more than enough to eat for the whole community.

Another time, the supply of olive oil used in the preparation of food, had completely run out. Olive oil, because of its healthy properties, was always given to sisters who were sick. Clare took the earthenware oil jar, washed and dried it by hand, and placed the empty vessel on the outside wall by the gate of the monastery, so that one of the brothers could take it on his errand to seek more oil. The brother was so devoted and anxious to help that, spying the vessel lying on the wall in the shade, he ran quickly to fetch it. Once again through the prayers of Clare, God had filled the jar with oil and the services of the brother were not needed on that particular day. The brother at first thought the sisters had been playing a trick on him; then on realising what had happened he exclaimed with great joy: "the jar was full".

The numbers in the Order were increasing far and wide, and as early as 1219 Clare sent her own Sister Agnes, as Abbess, to look after the monastery of Monticello near Florence. Widows foreign princesses of royal birth found peace in these enclosures of the Lord and by the end of the 1220s there were foundations of these "Damianites" at Rheims in France and in Spain.

Clare's own mother Ortolana, on becoming a widow, sold all her earthly possessions and property. She distributed the money amongst the poor and, clothed in the habit by Francis himself, joined San Damiano. Not long after, Clare's sister Beatrice, on reaching the age of eighteen, took her vows with the "new family". She would establish several new monasteries throughout Italy.

## Francis and Clare

Not long after Francis had given Clare and the "Order of Poor Ladies" his simple Rule, he sought Clare's councel with regards to his own ministry. He felt drawn to the contemplative life and for some time had been living the life of a hermit. Clare, who thought herself unworthy of the task, nevertheless took to prayer. God's answer was that Francis should give up his solitude and continue to proclaim the Gospel.

The only time Clare left San Damiano was at the invitation of Francis, at her insistence, to have a simple meal and "break bread" with him. This meal took place at St Mary of the Angels, the small Church, The Porziuncula, at the foot of Assisi where all those years ago Clare had received her poor habit. Clare took a sister with her to accompany her on this short journey. Throughout the meal, Francis, Clare and all of the companions were so rapt in heavenly ecstasy that it seemed to all the locals that a great fire, rising from within the church, was illuminating the night sky. The inhabitants of Assisi rushed to save the church and their woods and olive trees from being burnt to destruction, but discovered on arrival that it was the dinner party itself that was aglow with a "Divine Fire" fuelled by the flames of "Divine love".

In 1224 Francis received the Holy Stigmata, the five wounds of the crucified Lord in his hands, feet and side. For two years Clare looked after his intense sufferings, bandaging his wounds, wiping up the blood and making sandals for his feet, since even standing upright was a painful ordeal.

Francis knew that "Sister bodily death" was calling him, so he asked to be near the Church of San Damiano that he had built himself and to see Clare and the sisters. He remained in the precincts of the monastery, living in a small hut built out of mud and straw. During these days Clare's own bodily pains and infirmities began and would last until the end of her own life. During this period Francis composed not only his famous "Canticle of Brother Sun" but also another Song, written for his beloved sisters:

Listen, Little Poor Ladies, whom the Lord has called
who have come together from all parts of the world;
Live in loyal devotion to one another,
so that you die in obedience.
Do not look to the life outside;
because the life of the Holy Spirit is better.
In great love I beg you, use what God has given you
for your needs, with wise discretion.

All those of you who are afflicted with sickness
and all who care for them,
may you bear all this in peace.
For you will see how precious are such burdens,
because each of you will be crowned queen in heaven
with the Virgin Mary.

Francis' last days were spent in the Porziuncula
dictating spiritual letters and for Clare he wrote his last
piece of counsel:

"I, Brother Francis, want to follow the life and poverty
of Our Most High Lord Jesus Christ and of His Most
Holy Mother and to persevere in this to the end. And I
beg you, my ladies, and advise you always, that you live
in this most holy way of life and poverty. And guard
yourselves very much, in case by the teachings or advice
of anyone else you depart from this way of life".

On 3rd October 1226, an hour after sunset, Francis
died. Clare had one final request: to see Francis just one
last time. This was granted and the funeral procession
took a detour via San Damiano on its journey to Assisi.
His body was laid close to the choir grille window.
Clare was ill and allowed herself to be carried to the
small opening so that she could kiss the stigmatic
wound in Francis' hand and say farewell. From this
point onwards, Clare, who was known by all as "The

Little Plant" of St Francis, would blossom to new heights. Clare would meditate for long hours on the "original poverty" of the infant Jesus, the Babe of Bethlehem, wrapped in the poverty of the manger. This and much of what we know of the inner life of Clare, was to be beautifully revealed by her own hand in her famous preserved writings.

## THE SPIRITUALITY OF CLARE

### Her letters

In Cologne, Germany, there lived a very holy young girl called Ermentrude who led a virtuous life. After her parents died, she asked God what her vocation should be. By divine will and with advice from her Dominican priest, she set off to seek out a community of virgins. After many days of travelling she arrived in Belgium, in the delightful city of Bruges. Feeling that this was her journey's end, Ermentrude found favour with the city's inhabitants. Many young girls came to join her makeshift community and very quickly Ermentrude found herself in charge of a growing group of new, pure, 'Disciples of Christ'.

Not having any religious Rule, Ermentrude prayed for guidance and heard God say, "Take for your model, the virgin of Assisi". Ermentrude wrote to Clare asking for her advice.

It would have been very easy for Clare to despatch an Abbess to Bruges to oversee the development of this new community. However, Clare, the humble handmaid, recognised that this new flock would be best served from within and wrote a beautiful letter with some simple yet profound words. Clare's letters and other writings were written from deep within her heart. As we examine them more closely, it as though they could have been addressed to anyone, even to ourselves, in our contemporary world.

The faithfulness of Clare was a great virtue and being "faithful to Him", to Jesus, would, with the daily labours of this world, lead to that "Crown of Everlasting Life". What Clare promises for all is really quite uncomplicated: dedicate your life, your work, your recreation to God in all humility and "He will repay you", and "the reward will be eternal".

Clare would spend long hours "meditating on the mysteries of the cross and the passion of our Lord and the anguish of Mary standing beneath the Cross" and asks us to do the same. We are reminded to be "vigilant" and to beware of deceit in its many forms, to close our eyes and ears to flattery and temptations of the world. It is in prayer, "praying for one another's burdens that we fulfill Christ's laws".

Clare's letter to Ermentrude so filled her heart with joy and encouragement that the San Damiano Rule was introduced and faithfully followed. Later when Clare had passed away, Ermentrude travelled to Rome to ask the Pope for approval to extend the Order throughout Belgium and into the northern provinces of France so establishing even more monasteries.

It is hard to imagine today the importance of the art of letter writing. We barely have time to sit and gather our thoughts. Advice we wish to offer our families and friends seems to be motivated by exterior motives rather than those from within.

Clare wrote her first three letters to Agnes of Prague who would also be elevated to the sainthood. It is probable that many letters passed back and forth between these two saints and considerable time would pass between writing and receiving such letters as the delivery of any post would have been entrusted to the safe keeping of a priest or friar who would have had to undertake a long, hard journey, often by foot and only when an opportunity arose.

Agnes was born in Prague in 1200 and was the princess daughter of the King of Bohemia. From an early age she was educated in a monastery by St Hedwig and derived more pleasure from reading the life of saints than learning about how to fulfill her royal duties. As advances and offers of marriage from kings and princes arrived, Agnes, who longed for a life of prayer and solitude, turned to God in secret to consecrate her body to Him alone. Pope Gregory IX was called upon to intervene at one point and Agnes, under Papal protection, finally entered the monastery that she had already founded, the "Daughters of St Clare" in the city of Prague. This enclosure like Clare's would be her home until her death in her eightieth year.

Clare's letters to Agnes reveal the immense depth of love that stirred in her heart, love for Christ the Lord, and for poverty, which she mentions often: "I possess that which I most desire under heaven". Poverty is the treasure that Clare desired most, the possession that gave her greatest joy.

Clare explained that it was Jesus himself who was "despised, needy and poor in this world" and that those who are poor themselves can become "rich in Him by possessing the Kingdom of Heaven" and that one "cannot serve both God and money". Clare sought to store up a greater treasure in heaven and knew that eternal glory awaited those who "embraced her" (poverty). With her eyes fixed on the poor and crucified Christ she offered everything to God the Father in union with Jesus, to "Love Him who gave Himself totally out of love for you". In her life and letters, Clare and her sisters were sensitive to the daily needs of each person and took upon themselves the burdens, difficulties and sufferings of humanity.

As a handmaid of the Lord Clare was also united to Mary, Mother of Christ whom she asks us to love: "cling to His most sweet Mother Mary". It was Mary who offered her own virginal body to God and through the power of the Holy Spirit was enabled to "carry Jesus in the tiny enclosure of her sacred womb".

Clare's fourth and last known letter to Agnes was written many years later, in 1252, during the last months of Clare's life. Although more personal and reflective, it loses none of its dazzling brightness. She tells us of the great joy that we receive in participating in the Eucharist: "Happy, indeed, is the one permitted to share in this sacred banquet". For Clare joy becomes an antidote and shield against darkness and pain. In suffering "the poverty

of the child Jesus in the manger" and the poverty of the
cross, Clare was drawn deeper into union with Him. This
is the inspiration of Clare's devotion.

We are told of Jesus' great generosity, the promise of
the resurrection, "Whose fragrance will revive the dead,
and whose glorious vision will bless all the citizens of the
heavenly Jerusalem, because the vision of Him is the
splendour of everlasting glory". In speaking of the love of
Christ, Clare describes Christ himself as a mirror without
tarnish in which we see the reflection of ourselves and we
are asked to "Look into this mirror every day".

## The Rule for the Order of Poor Clares

For most of the time in San Damiano, the Poor Clares
had lived by the Rule or "Form of Life" that Francis had
taught them, with some new additions put in place by
two successive Popes. As many new monasteries started
to flourish in places near and far, Clare knew that she
would have to write her own Rule for the Order and so
became the first woman in the history of the Church to
compose a Religious Rule. The Rule was written over a
five-year period, from 1247. Its twelve chapters have
become a definitive Franciscan way of life. As the first
chapter states, the primary values are "to observe the
Holy Gospel of our Lord Jesus Christ, by living in
obedience, without anything (or property) of one's own,
and in chastity".

The ways of Jesus, were clearly to be put into practice: the sisters would "console the afflicted", "serve all those who were ill" and embrace the most absolute holy poverty "not being able to receive, or to have any possessions".

The Rule written in a very direct and concise manner and covers all aspects of a sister's vocation. It concludes with an admonition "always to observe the poverty and humility of our Lord Jesus Christ and of his Holy Mother and the Holy Gospel".

In her Rule Clare offers the way of holiness, nourished by prayer, that leads to contemplation of the very face of God. The opening of the heart to the Holy Spirit transforms the whole person to love and peace, and to the call to be a shining witness in the world.

## Clare's testament, prayers and blessing

When Francis died, Clare remained in this world a further twenty-seven years. She became the custodian and defender of Francis' example, principles and teachings. At the end of her life, Clare dictated what we would call a "Last Will and Testament". Her testament was recorded "In the name of the Lord", for which she gave "Thanks to God", for the Father's merciful love and kindness. Clare was convinced of the efficacy of reciprocal love in a community and said "Love one another with the charity of Christ, and let the love which you have in your hearts be shown outwardly by your deeds".

Clare is also attributed with composing the prayer recited each day, with much fervour and devotion, in "honour of the five wounds of our Lord", when she would fix her eyes on the poor and crucified Christ.

The famous 'Blessing of St Clare' which she gave to her sisters is a familiar prayer today, and is often used in a much shorter version of the original.

"I bless you during my life and after my death. I leave you all the blessings that I can give you, and I implore them from God, who lives and reigns world without end. Amen". Such a prayer assures us of Clare's intercession promised to us from heaven.

## SAN DAMIANO: THE LATER YEARS

### Penance, fasting and prayer

Clare's entire life was filled with penance, prayer and fasting, offered to her Saviour. Her form of penance and self-mortification was austere and, by the standards of today, may seem extreme. The habit she wore was coarse and rough and did little to keep her body warm. She had no use for shoes of any kind and her feet were always bare. Under her habit she wore a hair shirt, sometimes even preferring one made of sharp and prickly pigs' bristles. The ground served as Clare's bed: a layer of vines with a wooden block for a pillow. As her body weakened over time, Clare would allow her head a little straw and only much later, in obedience to Francis, would she succumb to using a straw-filled pillow.

So rigorous was her fasting and abstinence that only supernatural forces seemed to keep her alive. During the long lenten periods, Clare would eat nothing at all on Mondays, Wednesdays and Fridays and on the other days she would consume only bread and water, with a little wine on Sunday. Over the years such fasting deprived her body of strength and infirmities would set in. Eventually,

Francis and the Bishop instructed Clare to eat at least one and a half ounces of bread each day.

What Clare willingly lacked in bodily nourishment and sustenance was given back to her in contemplative prayer and praise to God. After Compline (night prayer) when all the other sisters had retired to their cells, Clare would continue watching throughout the night in prayer, often prostrate on the floor weeping floods of tears at the feet of Christ. On one such night, the devil attacked her taking the form of a small child. He warned her that so much crying would make her go blind, to which she replied "Those who shall see God will not be blind". The dark angel disappeared only to return later, just after midnight. He admonished her that all this weeping would make her brain go soft and that it would ooze through and deform her nose. Clare replied, "Those who serve the Lord need be afraid of nothing", at which the devil instantly vanished.

The community noted such joy and happiness in Clare that they would later testify during the canonization process that "her face was radiant when she came back from prayers...more beautiful than the sun".

Although the last to sleep each night, Clare made it her duty to rise first every morning, to light the lanterns and prepare Morning Prayer, with great charity and love for her sisters. She had another great love as well: the most holy Eucharist.

## The power of the Eucharist

Clare lived on that pure bread, the bread of heaven that was the real body of our Lord Jesus Christ. Today it may seem strange that according to the custom of the time, Clare could only receive the Eucharist seven times a year. It is also worth remembering that Francis never wanted to be ordained to the priesthood, and as a deacon was unable to celebrate Mass.

Pope John Paul II described Clare as a "eucharist, because from behind the enclosure, she raised up a continual thanksgiving to God in her prayer, praise, love and sacrifice, accepting everything and offering all to God in union with the Son, Jesus". Clare is often pictured standing, holding aloft a monstrance (the sacred vessel containing the Blessed Sacrament), defending her flock. In reality the event as depicted in art never occurred, but the truth contained in it is just as powerful.

In September 1240, Emperor Frederick II of Germany (also self-styled "King" of Naples and Sicily) having been excommunicated on more than one occasion, began ransacking those parts of Italy that were in close alliance with the Pope. In his anti-papal crusade he employed an army of lawless Saracens. Umbria and Assisi, known centres of Christian holiness, were among his main targets of war. His army reached the gates of Assisi and surrounded the monastery walls of San Damiano. The outer walls were breached and the bloodthirsty Saracens penetrated the confines of the cloisters. The sisters ran weeping and in fear to their holy mother Clare who was very ill. She told her daughters "Do not be afraid, for if the Lord is with us, the enemy cannot harm us". The sisters led Clare downstairs to the Blessed Sacrament, by which time the soldiers were trying to break down the refectory door to gain access to the inner sanctum. Clare took the silver pyx encased in ivory that contained the Blessed Sacrament and placed it between themselves and the enemy at the refectory door. Clare prostrated herself and with tears pleaded with God for her family to be delivered from the hands of the invading pagans. Immediately a child's voice was heard emanating from the pyx containing the real presence of Jesus: "I will protect you always". Clare asked that Assisi be defended and the reply came: "The city will be troubled, but shall be defended by my protection and your intercession". The hordes of Saracens retreated instantly overpowered by Clare's prayers.

In the following year Captain Vitalis of Aversa led Imperial troops against Assisi. The city was besieged and a under the menacing threat of attack. Clare dearly loved Assisi. She and her sisters covered their heads with ashes and pleaded for its liberation. The following morning, with God's merciful intervention, the enemy was beaten back never to return again.

The power of Clare's prayers was becoming increasingly well known. The defeat of human armies was a wonder, yet paled in comparison to defeating the army of darkness. A holy woman from Pisa came to Clare to give thanks that through her intercession, five demons had been cast out. On departing, the evil spirits confessed that the saint's prayers had fearfully tortured them.

Cardinal Hugolino, who later became Pope Gregory IX, also had great faith in Clare's prayers and would often recommend himself to her when he found himself in need. Such was her deep devotion to the Blessed Sacrament that in any crisis her natural response was to turn to the real presence of Jesus, and she never did so in vain.

## The sign of the cross

The six-foot Crucifix suspended over the altar at San Damiano is known as St Damian's Cross. It is the adopted Cross of the Franciscan Order. It is unusual as it is an icon painted in the Syrian style, rather than the usual attached, crucified figure. This was the very Cross that spoke to Francis and that drew Clare into great intimacy and understanding of God. Christ gazes out to the whole world, eyes wide open, crucified, yet not appearing sad or in pain. He welcomes those that look on him and announces to them the Paschal Mystery: his death, resurrection and ascension. There is a certain luminosity that clearly shines out from the colours painted by the unknown 12th century artist.

Clare's love for the crucified Jesus was well rewarded. Being so deeply inflamed with great love for the mystery of the cross, she received the gift of performing miracles simply by making the sign of the cross. Whenever the cross was signed over a sick person, they would be healed immediately.

Once Francis, knowing of this divine virtue, sent one his Brothers who was suffering from a form of insanity. Brother Stephen was "signed" and fell into a slumber to wake a little while later cured of his madness.

Three-year-old Mattiolo from Spoleto, had a pebble lodged in his nose. Nothing could remove it and he was close to suffocation. The boy was taken to Clare and the stone ejected itself with some force, once the sign was made over him. Another boy, from Perugia, whose eye was completely covered by a large sore was taken to San Damiano. On seeing him, Clare touched his eye and made the cross sign with her finger. She asked her religious sister and mother, Ortolana, to do the same. At once the child was cured of the ulcer and could see clearly again. Clare attributed the miracle to her mother, who deferred all praise back to her daughter.

The sign of the cross healed those among her own community. Sister Benvenuta had suffered for twelve years from malignant ulcers under her arm and elsewhere. The usual miraculous remedy healed the festering and discharging wounds. Sister Amata had for many months showed signs of dropsy fever and violent coughing and was restored to perfect health. Sister Christina who was deaf, and another Sister who had lost her speech, were both cured by Clare's saintly touch.

On one particular occasion the monastery infirmary was filling up with sick sisters. Clare paid a visit and made the sign of the cross in the air five times at which point all five sisters rose from their sick beds once the "remedy" had been applied. Clare drew from the pierced heart of Jesus, his healing power for those who were suffering. Her empathy and deep faith enabled Christ to heal those for whom she prayed.

Pope Gregory IX witnessed these signs on one of his visits to Assisi. He went to San Damiano to see Clare, as he wished to hear her speak of heavenly things. Baked bread rolls were brought from the kitchen to be blessed by the Holy Father who in turn asked Clare to bless them. Clare submitted, and made the sign of the cross over the small loaves: at once an imprint of the cross appeared on each loaf.

### Clare's love of Jesus and her sisters

Clare grieved daily over the Lord's Passion and taught her novices to do the same. As she contemplated the crucified Christ, her heart was filled with compassion and this overflowed to all around her and fired her prayers for the salvation of souls.

Clare led by example and often shed tears, in prayer, in the confines of her cell. So intense was her devotion to the five wounds of the crucified Christ that one day at three o'clock, the hour of the Passion, the devil came to her cell and beat her with brutal force, causing her eyes to fill with blood and bruising her face. This only made Clare engage more deeply in her acts of prayer to God.

As one Easter approached, Clare, again locked in the seclusion of her cell, meditated on the Last Supper. From Maundy Thursday until, the close of Good Friday, Clare remained transfixed in remembrance of the Lord's suffering: "All I want is to know Christ and the power of his resurrection and to share his sufferings by reproducing the pattern of his death" (*Phil* 3:10).

Clare instructed the sisters with discipline and love. She taught them to meditate on God alone, to forget their previous lives and homes in order to please Christ; to disregard the demands of the flesh, and to overcome the wickedness and snares of the evil one. She taught them to do manual labour and to learn how to speak little, and about only what was necessary.

Clare arranged for visiting preachers so that all could regularly hear the Word of God. She experienced such happiness during these sessions that one time a heavenly child appeared at her side, during one of the Brother's sermons. Light like the brilliance of the stars shone around her and she exuded a most intense, sweet fragrance. Sister Agnes of Spello witnessed the child Jesus embraced in Clare's arms, and heard his sweet voice: "My daughter, I am in the midst of you".

Clare understood God's humility and his compassion for the human race. Compassion for Clare was a constant self-emptying, whereby she made her heart available for those who suffered. Humility, often considered the foundation of the spiritual life, can involve a certain fearlessness. By relinquishing their self-reliance and all forms of security, a person may come to know they are in fact nothing and so rely totally on God. Clare showed this fearlessness in many ways: by leaving home, confronting the enemy, the devil, by politely and respectfully opposing Popes and Cardinals who tried to persuade her to accept land and revenues. "I will never in any way wish to be absolved from following Christ". Clare remained faithful to her ideals, following her Lord in complete trust.

Clare was always united to God, and compassionate in the way she attended to the sisters' welfare and needs. She would allow a less rigorous routine for any of her children who were unable to cope with the strict observances. If a sister was tempted, Clare would console her with tears and even place herself at her feet if they were melancholy or sorrowful. The community had a great affection and respect for their Superior and tried to follow her way of perfection.

## CLARE'S ILLNESS AND LAST DAYS

### Clare's long infirmity and work

For almost half her life, Clare suffered from a mysterious illness that deprived her of physical strength, and finally left her a bedridden invalid. Nothing, however, seemed to trouble her and she was never heard to utter a single complaint about her sickness or the poverty that she had embraced. So great was her joy to serve the Lord, she exclaimed: "They say we are too poor, but can a heart which possesses the infinite God be truly called poor?"

One Christmas eve, as Clare was confined to her bed, Jesus came to her in her suffering. At midnight, sad that she would miss the joyful celebrations, Clare suddenly heard the beautiful music and hymns being sung in the Church of St Francis. Normally this was impossible because of the church's distance from San Damiano. This miracle was surpassed, when Clare was given the grace to actually witness the proceedings in the Church of St Francis, seeing the crib and the holy infant Jesus lying in the manger; she was transported to the Church to receive Holy Communion before being returned to her bed.

In 1251 Clare's medical condition gradually turned the more grave and she found herself confined to her small bed. The rigours of her austere way of life were now beginning to take their toll and the sickness and fatigue had weakened her considerably. Yet even from her sick bed she continued to work for God. Heavy manual tasks were beyond her but using those fingers that healed so many with her sign of the cross and touch, Clare managed to spin dozens of corporals. These were wrapped in small silk cases and given to the Franciscan Brothers to distribute to the poorer churches in the surrounding Umbrian mountains, hills and valleys.

One day Sister Amata noticed a great change in her mother Clare. Instead of appearing pale and drawn, Clare's features beamed with great happiness and when questioned about this remarkable change, Clare replied: "How can I help rejoicing, since at this moment, I hold in my arms my dearest Lord who is the joy of my soul". Christian joy was her triumphal virtue, which drew its energy from victory over suffering. Like all gifts of grace this joy came to her soul from heaven, mediated by Our Lord. At that moment Jesus revealed his presence to Amata also and she gazed upon him with such intense joy.

### Visit of the Pope and confirmation of the Rule

Throughout Clare's sickness, nothing but prayer, praise and thanksgiving came from her lips. Although death seemed but a short time away, God still had further favours to grant his daughter. Between 1244 and 1251,

Pope Innocent IV, due to hostilities with Frederick II in Italy, had taken residence in Lyon, France. Now a Benedictine nun in Clare's original monastery at San Paolo had a remarkable vision in which she saw the sick Clare lying in bed. Those gathered around her were sobbing, when a beautiful lady appeared saying: "My daughters, do not weep and mourn for the one who looks dead, for she will live and not die until the Lord and his disciples visit her". Not long after this revelation, the Pontiff left France. Italy was now at peace and Pope Innocent IV headed south to Perugia. Hearing of Clare's serious condition, Cardinal Raynaldus, who would become the next Pope, rushed from Perugia to see Clare, his close friend and counsellor. He administered Holy Communion and commended Clare and her sisters to God. Clare dearly wanted the Pope to finally confirm and approve the Rule for her Order in writing. The Cardinal faithfully promised to do for her all he could and took his leave back to Perugia. Another year passed and Clare, still clinging to life, waited. The Papal party then took up temporary residence in Assisi for the Basilica of St Francis was now complete and to be consecrated. The representative of the Lord had arrived at last with his "disciples".

Clare longed to be free of her mortal body and meet her Lord in the heavenly mansions. With her strength draining fast from her frail and weak frame, Pope Innocent and his entourage of Cardinals made haste to visit her. On entering San Damiano, he went straight to the infirmary where Clare lay on her sick bed. He held out his hand but Clare wished to kiss his feet. Moved by such reverence the Pope climbed on to a wooden stool and Clare was able to turn slightly to one side and impress her kiss on his foot.

Clare asked the Holy Father for pardon and remission of all her sins. The Pope, with hands raised, gave her absolution and an apostolic blessing. Clare then received Jesus Christ in Holy Communion. Clare asked the Pope for the one favour that only he could give: written Papal approval of the Rule that she herself wrote for the Order of Poor Ladies.

When all the dignitaries and visitors had left, Clare raised her tear-filled eyes to heaven and said to her devoted sisters "Praise the Lord with me, my daughters; for on this day Christ has been pleased to grant me a great favour, which nothing in heaven or on earth can fail to compensate. Today, I have received the Most High God in Holy Communion and have been made worthy to see His Vicar on earth".

In her final three weeks, her community gathered around her bedside forsaking sleep, finding comfort and relief only in weeping tears day and night. Clare's sister, the Abbess Agnes, was recalled from the monastery of Monticello near Florence to be at her side; overwhelmed with grief she implored Clare not to depart this life without taking her as well. Clare's final gift of prophecy was revealed by the words, "It pleases God that I go shortly. Stop your own weeping sister, for you shall pass to the Lord not long after I am gone, and before your death the Lord will grant you a great consolation". "St Agnes" died a saintly death in November 1253, just three months later.

For seventeen days Clare was unable to take any food yet she was still able to encourage all who called upon her "to be strengthened in the service of Christ". To Brother Raynaldo who asked her to be patient in her martyrdom of suffering, Clare replied: "Ever since I have known the grace of Our Lord Jesus Christ no suffering has been bothersome, no penance too severe, no infirmity has been hard".

Clare asked for the Lord's Passion to be read to her. She recommended her holy daughters of poverty to be ever mindful of the benefits that come from praise and thanksgiving. Two of Francis' companions came: Brother Leo, confessor and advisor, who kissed the dying saint's bed. Brother Angelo, Francis' first companion, consoled the rest of the nuns.

On Saturday 10 August 1253, as Clare lay dying and just holding on to life, her ardent desire to have her Rule confirmed was realized. The Papal Bull signed in Assisi the day before, was rushed over to Clare by a group of Friars. It was placed in her hands and in great weakness Clare raised it to her lips with great devotion. She could now finally go in peace to meet her creator.

## A holy death and burial

During the night of Friday 9 August, the sisters keeping a bedside vigil testified that they heard Clare talking very lucidly and calmly to her own soul, in what can be described as her own Magnificat: "Go forth in peace, for you will have good company on your journey". She continued, "Go forth, for he who created you has sanctified you, and, having protected you always, has loved you with the tender love that a mother gives her child". Clare then prayed: "Thank you Lord for having created me".

Throughout the night Clare prayed her favourite devotion to the Five Wounds of Christ. She told (another) Sister Agnes, in her final words: "Precious in the sight of the Lord is the death of his holy ones". During these final hours of passage, a miraculous vision occurred. Sister Benvenuta gazed towards the monastery door and beheld a procession of Virgins dressed in white robes and wearing golden crowns upon their heads. Amidst them walked one greater, more beautiful, whose crown was more resplendent, like a thurible from which came forth a brilliant luminesence that turned the night into day. The Blessed Virgin Mary approached Clare's bed and leaning towards her most lovingly, took her and embraced her. Mary then covered Clare with the most exquisite and delicate cloth and the two Maidens of the Lord became as one, indistinguishable from one another and the room became radiantly adorned. The summer evening light of Monday 11 August was starting to fade. It was the great feast of St Ruffino, Assisi's patron, and Sister Filippa, Clare's life long friend, has described how Clare, without the darkness of sin, passed peacefully from this life to the Lord.

The news of Clare's death brought the populace of Assisi running to San Damiano. The mayor and the knights of the city kept vigil around their treasured lady. The following day, the Pope, Cardinals and Priests came to celebrate the funeral Mass. Pope Innocent IV was eager to canonize her instantly and had to be persuaded by his assistant, Cardinal Raynaldus, to wait until reflection of her true holiness had been made.

Clare's earthly remains were carried on a bier and buried in the Church of St George, by Assisi's eastern gate.

## Cause, miracles and canonisation

Within weeks of Clare's death, Pope Innocent IV opened the promotion and examination of her cause for canonisation. The postulator was the Bishop of Spoleto who was assisted by the Franciscan Friars, Leo and Angelo among others. The Bishop investigated and questioned the citizens of Assisi and others who had either known Clare personally or had benefitted from her intercession or miracles. His interviews were conducted at the Church of San Paolo in the centre of Assisi. Thirteen sisters from the monastery of San Damiano testified under oath in great detail regarding the sanctity of their Mother Abbess. The inhabitants of Assisi and surrounding towns were able to recall Clare's life, her childhood, her conversion, her love for those in need. Those who gave testimony recalled her great love of the poor, her "honesty, kindness and humility" and "compassion for people's body and souls."

During the examination process, many miracles were recorded and attributed after her death. A boy from Perugia suffered from possession and would throw himself in the fire and perform many acts of disfiguring violence against his own body. His father placed him on Clare's tomb, and he was immediately freed from the diabolical attacks which never returned. Two other women and a youth from France with similar symptoms were also cured at Clare's tomb; their paralysis was cured, their lives restored to normal.

A young man suffering from daily epileptic fits and contracted legs was placed by the tomb and on the third day his leg was heard to "snap" back into place. He was also healed of his epilepsy. Another Perugian man about to lose his hand that had been crushed by a stone had his hand restored to its former healthy condition. Another man had wasted almost to a skeleton, bent double and hardly able to walk. He also was cured by the merits of the holy virgin Clare.

Two boys disabled from birth, could only move by crawling. Their lameness was cured by the power of God, through Clare.

Two other small children were saved from the jaws of death; they had been carried away by wolves into the forests. The prayers of their mothers to Clare did not fall on empty ears, and the wolves let loose their prey.

Those with tumours, cancers of the throat were also made well again. One girl who suffered numerous painful lumps, saw them gradually soften and disappear completely. A similar miraculous healing of the throat had occurred to Sister Andrea of San Damiano in Clare's own lifetime.

Many other remarkable miracles were recorded. On one occasion Clare herself appeared over three nights in a dream to a blind man who lived many miles away. She asked him to visit her so that he should see again. After falling asleep at her tomb, he was awakened by her voice, and realised at once that he could see clearly.

Not long after her death Clare's fame as a miracle worker spread. It fell upon the shoulders of Cardinal Raynaldus who had become the new Pope, Alexander IV, to examine the extraordinary life of Clare. The commission concluded and confirmed "Clare, while living was a most shining and resplendent example of every virtue and that in death was worthy of admiration for real and proven miracles". The commission agreed that Clare deserved to be glorified on earth, since God had glorified her in heaven.

Clare was canonised within two years of her death. Forty miles south-east of Rome, at the cathedral in Agnani thousands flocked to witness this great celebration. In the opening sentence of his Bull of Canonisation, Alexander proclaimed that Clare was "a clear and shining light" that "now shines in heaven"...and on earth. His address spoke of her "brilliance", "the princess of the poor". Before the gathered multitude, the Holy Pontiff raised the holy virgin, Clare, to the ranks of the saints.

## THE ASSISI OF ST CLARE TODAY

### St Clare and the Basilica

Clare's remains were interned in the Church of St George in the eastern part of Assisi, rather than San Damiano, as protection against would-be thieves. In medieval times it was not uncommon for the bodies or relics of saints to be "kidnapped" for veneration elsewhere. The Church of St George however was small, even too small to hold the vast number of pilgrims who were travelling from not just all over of Italy, but from much further afield. As a matter of duty the inhabitants of Assisi constructed a building befitting of a great saint. Seven years later, in 1260, the new Church and monastery were completed and on 3 October, the feast of St Francis, Pope Alexander IV presided over the translation of Clare's body to its new resting place. The Community of Sisters also transferred from San Damiano to their new monastery attached to the new cathedral, where they could be close to their beloved Saint and Mother Clare.

When Clare's tomb was opened seven years after her death, her body was found to be totally incorrupt, as though she had just fallen asleep. The body was placed in a stone coffin beneath the High Altar, the deep cavity being sealed with solid brick and masonry, again as protection from marauding trophy hunters. The Cathedral was dedicated to St Clare on the same day, and five years later, in 1265, it was consecrated by Pope Clement IV, and the holy shrine became the Basilica of St Clare. (It is here that the original San Damiano Cross is kept). Nearly six hundred years later, in 1850 the Holy See gave permission for the tomb to be opened and a new place of veneration was found within the basilica. It took seven full days and nights to excavate the stone coffin and on Sunday, 22 September, the tomb was opened. The metal straps were cut and the lid was slowly raised using a system of rope pulleys. Clare's body was found to be intact and in a dry and preserved state. On her breast, resting still, lay a laurel branch and a crown of flowers.

A large crypt was hewn out of the stone floor, with a magnificent chapel and crystal reliquary. In 1872 Clare's remains were moved from the nun's choir to the new shrine, under the guidance of Pope Pius IX, for public veneration. She can be seen clothed in her habit, with her face, hands and feet bare.

In 1893, there was a remarkable find. Whilst her habit was being rearranged, the original written Rule for the Order, written in her own hand, was found in the folds of her mantle.

The entrance to the crypt is by stairs from the centre of the Basilica, and on the way down you also have the opportunity to view a large array of relics that include St Clare's long golden locks of hair, the hair shirt, mantle and habit that she wore. Descending further, you come to St Clare herself, resting for all to see. In 1980, having been exposed for so long, her body had begun to show signs of deterioration and it was decided to encase it in a perfectly measured, ceramic, lifelike moulding. What we see today is the body of St Clare, resting on a slightly raised wooden pillow in a more simple crystal glass coffin, holding flowers.

### Walking in her footsteps to San Damiano

Assisi is a preserved city and pilgrims find themselves transported back to the twelfth century. Little has changed and it is very easy to walk the paths, squares and ways of the saints who lived there. Traffic is mostly prohibited and Assisi remains the domain of the pedestrian. Many visitors flock to the three-tiered Basilica of St Francis often leaving little time to visit the Basilica of St Clare. To really explore the spirituality of a place like Assisi takes time, and at least two or three full days are needed.

The Monastery and Church of San Damiano is reached by a relatively short, steep and very scenic walk from the eastern gate of Assisi. At this point we are reminded that Clare's love embraced all creation and she would tell those sisters serving outside the walls "to praise God when they saw beautiful trees, flowers and bushes; and likewise, always praise him in all things when they saw all peoples and creatures".

The monastery today is looked after by the Franciscan Friars, and could well be described as the most perfect haven of peace and tranquillity. Set amid olive groves, this is the centre of St Clare's world. To walk and sit in the cloisters, garden and courtyard, with views of the surrounding countryside, is inspiring, enlightening and calming. The chapel, (Mass is still celebrated here early each morning), the refectory and St Clare's cell, all with their original benches and tables, remain just as they did eight hundred years ago and provide a physical link to the past. Today this certainly remains a centre of spirituality, a place to reflect quietly and to be still: "You will reveal the path of life to me, give me unbounded joy in your presence" (*Psalm* 16:11, Mass on the feast of St Clare).

## St Clare's patronage and legacy

The Feast Day of Saint Clare falls on 11 August. Originally it was 12 August, because although Clare died on the 11th, that was the feast day of Assisi's patron, Saint Ruffino. St Clare is not only a Patron to Assisi, she is also the Patron Saint of eye disease (her miracles described earlier), and the Patron of embroiderers (needle work). In 1958 Pope Pius XII declared St Clare the patron saint of television. This was due to one Christmas when, too ill to leave her bed, Clare saw projected on her wall, and heard, the whole of the Midnight Mass taking place miles away.

Clare in her own lifetime saw the foundation of 153 monasteries of her Order. Today there are 900 monasteries in 76 countries with 20,000 Poor Clare Sisters.

St Clare has a lot to teach us today and shines as a lantern to help us find our steps along the way. Clare would definitely shy away from the title of "Great Saint". Her greatness lay in the way she was so humble: "Do all that has to be done without complaining or arguing and then you will be innocent and genuine,…and you will shine in the world like bright stars" (*Phil* 2:14-16). St Clare asks us "to strive always to imitate the way of holy simplicity and humility".

# SELECTED BIBLIOGRAPHY

All Scripture texts are taken from *The Jerusalem Bible*, 1966, Darton, Longman and Todd Ltd, with grateful acknowledgement by the CTS.

*The Life of Saint Clare* by Thomas Celano (1255-61). Translated by Fr. Paschal Robinson OFM, Dolphin Press, 1910.

*The Princess of Poverty: Saint Clare of Assisi and The Order of Poor Ladies* by Fr Marianus Fiege OFM Cap, 1900. Published by the Poor Clare Monastery, Evansville, Indiana.

*Saint Clare of Assisi* by Sr Chiara Augusta Lainati OSC, 1994, Edizioni Porziuncola.

*Clare of Assisi: Early Documents*. Revised and Expanded Edition by Fr Regis J. Armstrong OFM Cap, 1993, Franciscan Institute Publications and the Paulist Press.

*Jubilee Guide to Assisi*, 1999, Libreria Editrice Vaticana.

*Letters on Saint Clare of Assisi*, by Pope John Paul II, (1993 & 2003), Vatican Archive.

# Informative Catholic Reading

We hope that you have enjoyed reading this booklet.

If you would like to find out more about CTS booklets we'll send you our free information pack and catalogue.

Please send us your details:

Name ...................................................................

Address ...............................................................

............................................................................

............................................................................

Postcode ..............................................................

Telephone.............................................................

Email ..................................................................

Send to:    CTS, 40-46 Harleyford Road,
            Vauxhall, London
            SE11 5AY

Tel: 020 7640 0042
Fax: 020 7640 0046
Email: info@cts-online.org.uk

# CTS Great Saints Series

Anthony of Padua *(B 679)*

Benedict - Patron of Europe *(B 682)*

Charles Borromeo *(B 685)*

Clare of Assisi *(B 686)*

Francis Xavier *(B 688)*

Ignatius Loyola *(B 687)*

Louis Marie de Montfort *(B 680)*

Padre Pio *(B 669)*

Patrick *(B 666)*

Philip Neri *(B 670)*

Thérèse of Lisieux *(B 204)*

*Also:*

Message of Assisi *(D 658)*

# Clare
## *of* Assisi

### *CTS Great Saints Series*

In renouncing the world of her time and embracing poverty, Clare risked everything to be a disciple of Christ. She was not only inspired by her contemporary, St Francis, but in turn gave him counsel and at one stage even nursed him. So great was her impact on Christendom, that by her death in 1253 over 150 convents of the Poor Clare Order of nuns had been established. Her inspiring life, writings and legacy - and their modern day relevance - are considered here.

ISBN 1-86082-354-8

 **CTS**

B 686          £1.95

# PEACE & WAR
## n today's world

What the Catholic
Church thinks
and why

y Craig M. White

# CTS Publications

CTS booklets explain the faith, teaching and life of the Catholic Church. They are based on Sacred Scripture, the Second Vatican Council documents, and the *Catechism of the Catholic Church*. Our booklets provide authentic Catholic teaching; they address issues of life and of truth which are relevant to all. They aim to inform and educate readers on the many issues that people have to deal with today.

In addition, CTS nurtures and supports the Christian life through its many spiritual, liturgical, educational and pastoral books. As Publisher to the Holy See, CTS publishes the official documents of the Catholic Church as they are issued.

The CTS is one of the oldest and one of the few sizable publishers of exclusively Catholic publications; its booklets are completely reliable. CTS seeks to communicate and celebrate the riches of the Catholic faith to all.

*website: www.cts-online.org.uk*

*All rights reserved. Published 2011 by The Incorporated Catholic Truth Society, 40-46 Harleyford Road, London SE11 5AY Tel: 020 7640 0042 Fax: 020 7640 0046. © 2011 The Incorporated Catholic Truth Society.*

*ISBN 978 1 86082 715 0*